His Cheer Leader

Author: Dr. Felicia S. Cunningham

His Cheer Leader

FOREWORD

Dr. Felicia S. Cunningham, I decree that this book will help the nations.

I pray that this book helps you realize how important you are and that you are not just here to exist. Your pain is your praise. Your dilemmas and experiences help you know more than just His name. He loves you and so do I.

As you read this book allow the Spirit of the Lord to minister to you. As you open your spiritual eyes and understanding, open your heart, your soul and your spirit to receive the healing God has just for you. See yourself as Father God sees you, complete in HIM!

For this day you will arise into your new destiny, purpose and day…

Dr. M. L. Cunningham

CONTENTS

"His Cheer Leader"

What does it take to be a woman who is called and ordained by God to be virtuous, walking in a kingdom mindset, authority, power and leadership while backing and supporting a powerful prolific, prophetic man of God whom God has entrusted you to birth in the spirit to a destiny He has been ordained and called to from the mouth of Almighty God from the day he was deposited into his mother's womb? I'm talking about your soul mate, your confidant. The jewel, the diamond in a rough and precious promise God has ordained for you to walk with in life…

I wanted to take the time to encourage women who are married or who will soon be married or who are believing God for their mate to be encouraged knowing that your prayers and labor of love for your mate is not in vain. If you are not married, I would like to calibrate on you getting a deeper connection with God so that you will be prepared for your promise and head (Husband). Your job as a single lady and woman of God now is to set a standard of living so that your prayers will not be hindered.

James 5:16 (KJV), *"The effectual fervent prayer of a righteous man (woman) avail much...."*

As you have set the standard of being committed to God and have faithfully been married to the Lord, you have come to be seasoned and obedient to the voice of God. Now, after you have become sensitive to His Spirit and have come to know His voice, it is time that you begin to pray for your promised mate and to pre-birth him in the Spirit now, using intercession and travail as Hannah prayed for conception and pre-dedicated Samuel to the Lord for Kingdom purposes before he was conceived and birthed forth out of the Spirit into her womb and then into the physical.

The Single Cheerleader

If you are single right now, you have the ability, being a daughter of God, to cheer your mate on in the Spirit having not laid eyes on him in the physical.

By you praying for his success and his eyes to open to catch and see the vision of God right now for his life, it will be impossible for him to miss you or to pass you by in your ready and right now season. It also will be impossible for you to not see the Ishmael before the Isaac, meaning you won't accept an invite from some man who God has not ordained for you. You will recognize the quarterback you prayed for as he enters the field for the ballgame, meaning warfare, God's Kingdom vs. Satan's.

The best cheerleader is one who practices cheering at home, on and off the field or court, with a passion and expectation, one who sees herself cheering in a vision and while encouraging other cheerleaders, showing no hate or jealousy cheering as if on the field during her own game even if there is no game or game season. While she waits for game season, the vision for her Boaz continues to last as she continues to grow into a perfectionist at cheering. She cheers and exercises her gift of motivation and exaltation while waiting on the season where her practice becomes perfect and the love that cast out all fear. While moving into position mentally and physically, from mirror to mirror, glory to glory in her home, she examines her steps, all the time cheering, and making intercession from the depths of her innermost being, and shouting as if she was already in game season on the field.

By her continual practicing out of season, all the while preparing for game season to arrive by her labor and persistence of being focused while patiently awaiting the arrival of game season, this consistent and confident cheerleader now has become a perfectionist at cheering and a mature stable minded cheerleader. She is ready for game time, attracting on the field, not only the quarterback, but the team she cheers with showing them that hope and belief while steadfast in the season of waiting pays off; even, when it seems like the wait is forever and dreams and unanswered prayer is not coming into fruition.

With all of her hard practice and dedication to cheering, she is now ready for promotion to becoming head cheerleader receiving new revelation to build on what has already been laid. Can't you see her yelling and cheering, saying go, go, go? Even though she has not known the boys on the field for long and they do not know her hard out of season struggle of practicing her cheers with a passion. Now with compassion and that same passion she pushes them to run on with her faith and belief; with her mouth believing that her words and body motions will help them progress and win, even if their faith may be in a temporary moment of disbelief because of the hardships and opposition of the game.

She has seen from the beginning that even if the game looks to be fatal or in disarray, she would still keep encouraging herself and her teammates with her mouth speaking and screaming Go, Go, Go, You are more than a conqueror! You should know! With her spirit whether snow, sun, rain, or hail, she is determined to push, scream and yell. She may not at the moment be able to be in her teammates' ear, but with her mouth and powerful words while she motions her body pushing cheers, she pushes them closer and nearer till the end of the game. Whether victory or losing, she still speaks encouragement for their spirit to hear, binding and rebuking the bitter embarrassment, and inner pain with pleasant positive speaking, declaring victory is still to gain, so have no shame.

Go, go, go, go, you are more than a conqueror! You should know! A real cheerleader cheers and focuses on her call and duty to cheer. Even when the game is over, she still holds her faith and duty and call to cheer. As women of virtue standing on the front line, there are many things we are called to stand in and uphold while remaining in an unmovable position to be encouraged while yet encouraging ourselves and others while waiting on God's time and plan to birth forth the promises of His true God-sent man. The responsibility is that you must keep a mindset to always be prepared to cheer. Before I laid eyes on my husband, the Lord had shown me in a vision through prayer how he would look. He also showed me how he had some hurt and pain from his past and that he would need someone while enroute to his destiny in God to cheer for him. Not when just the good had occurred, but even when there were mistakes. I never badgered my husband. I just told him it will be better the next time if he failed. Even when the Lord had me pre-warn him and he did not listen at the time, I still prayed for him with my emotions screaming inside of me wanting to yell. **As a cheerleader, emotions can't get involved.** You must remember the principal and by laws of the game. God's word!

As a cheerleader, there is responsibility to direct the quarterback to run, run, run, because she sees the opposition stealing in close, trying to knock him down so he would fumble the ball. They want to steal it and run trying to make a touchdown. There will be times when you will have to cheer although you are tired. It may seem like the vision for you and your mate in God is not near or when it looks like the offense, the enemy has taken the blessing and disappeared.

YOU must continue to cheer!

I remember having to go through a trial with my husband and some ex-church members who were causing confusion in trying to get him delayed and off focus from the vision God gave him. When I say drama and confusion, these certain individuals did all they could do to try and destroy my man, my husband, and my promise. You know how church folks do when they can't have their way. They will take a truth, twist it into a lie, and scandalize the pastor's name, trying to defame their character and name. Whether true or not in what they had to say or portray, God sent me my quarterback and the game I knew we had to play! I had to encourage my husband to go and get the Super Bowl ring despite the side snipers who were aiming to try and kill him, the vision and the seed of righteousness God placed in him. Now if I were carnal as my husband would say, I would have thrown in the towel or maybe even found some of these supposed to have been true Christians and put them in place, but as I knew in advance through my prayer life and studying the game. **"Yes," cheerleaders do have to study each game.** It helps you to get ready for the unexpected. God showed me how the enemy would try to make an interception when unexpected.

Since I knew that the devil is against unity and God's plan, I allowed the Spirit of God to lead me and guide me leading me into each and every situation. The waiting was a faith and character builder, while God was positioning my husband and me to condemn the tongues of these enemies and be the next giant killers. Yet, there also was a test to see if I was a determined, committed, seasoned cheerleader. "Could I handle the game and cheer through all four quarters?"

I remembered having to think back when I was a single cheerleader on what I would do if something bad drew near. All the while knowing I was called to uplift and cheer, not just for my husband but for other bold influential women who would come behind me, being that example that they too can cheer their mate on when storms or trials draw near.

Especially coming from an out of season cheerer to a seasoned cheerer, knowing even if it is game time and the charades draw near, you still have to stay focused and to cheer. No one can cheer for your mate like you can and will! They can pat him on his back and say job well done. They can say go get him buddy and pretend they cheer him on, but they really don't. But, when the tempest arises and the winds begin to blow that is when he'll find out and you will see the man standing to cheer will be the one God has assigned, and that is you! You are left alone standing to cheer for him and for you with no questions on what to do, as you have prepared for your season and you are excited to cheer.

The Married Cheerleader

If you are married and your mate is not saved or you have a mate who is a minister or clergy, your job as a woman of God and a woman called to virtue is to support and cheer your mate to the for front of the line and stand with him through every battle and war. How do you do this while waiting on the answer and arrival of God's word to manifest in your marriage? It is called remembering where your mate came from and what your mate came out of and how you received him in his imperfect state. You chose to take on the responsibility of helping him to achieve every God-given vision and desire and wanting accomplished. It means loving him and continuously falling in love with him and seeing the God in him as you did when you first met him. He promised you some things and had a vision that seemed too good to be true, yet sounding worthwhile, believing him to accomplish them while waiting believing in the manifestations. The same way you vowed to love him in the good is the same way you must remember to encourage him and yourself in the bad while waiting on your promises to manifest from the spiritual to the material.

While waiting you are your mate's biggest cheerleader!

When God sees the negative, He calls forth the positive. **Genesis 1:1-5 (KJV)** *"In the beginning God created the heaven and the earth. And the earth was without form, and void, and darkness [was] upon the face of the deep. And the Spirit of God moved upon the face of the waters. And God said, Let there be light: and there was light. And God saw the light, that [it was] good: and God divided the light from the darkness. And God called the light Day, and the darkness he called Night."*

He never gets weary in waiting on us for salvation, in getting us into the place of sincerely receiving His only begotten Son, who He sent forth as the ultimate trailblazer to prepare the way for us and becoming the ultimate sacrifice for us. God reminds Himself of who He is which is Truth, Creator, and all powerful. Even God, looking back, encourages Himself of how He has built and labored with His word to accomplish and fulfill the vision He has had for the world and mankind.

So, you, being a daughter of God must know the first tool God has given you which is your faith and secondly to plow in the Spirit believing and speaking that which is not to be as though it was.

Romans 4:17 (NET), *(as it is written, **"I have made you the father of many nations"**). "He is our father in the presence of God whom he believed---the God makes the dead alive and summons the things that do not exist as though they already do."*

Calling and birthing your husband's mandate on his life, saved or unsaved, as it has to manifest for God's glory. What you speak must manifest if it is aligned with the perfect plan and will of God. No, you don't have to be in your mate's ear and he does not have to hear you speaking this life into the atmosphere. Your desires must become God's desire. Once they both align, then you will see manifestation while being patient. Many have quoted the following scripture,

Psalms 37:4 (NASB), *"Delight yourself in the Lord; And He will give you the desires of your heart."*

True indeed, but when you are in love with God then you are in a place of acceptance to His total plan. I will give you an example, my husband and I believed God for a new truck. We believed within ourselves that it was time for a trade but God believed something else. We had no finances but the faith that could move mountains. The one thing we lacked was the permission from God. The car we drove was a bright yellow 2004 Chevy two door Cavalier. Boy did we get attention! People were amazed at how we squeezed in that car with our four girls along with a car seat. We really had to have faith for God to keep us from not getting pulled over by officers, and, that He would keep His healing power upon and around our lives. After some rides of going to and from church or just driving from one city to another, my back and legs were really hurting me, at times! Now, when God finally allowed us to get another vehicle, it was a year later in the same month we wanted to purchase a SUV.

The truck we wanted was a pretty green, had television, a sunroof and seventy-five thousand miles on it with a V8 engine. The truck God ordained for us was the same type of truck but on another lot, about an hour and a half away. It was the same color, same model, and had lower miles, about thirty three thousand less to be exact. The other truck we wanted we were willing to settle for the price and believe God. Now all the time we had prayed we asked God for His perfect will and that He would give us favor and He sure did - unexpected favor. Once we went home and prayed about the truck we wanted, the Lord directed us to another place an hour away. Being obedient, my husband and I went on blind faith.

When we arrived to the car place not only did the truck match the one we wanted from the inside out, but purpose was behind our arrival. Not only did my husband and I purchase the truck through the favor of God but we were able to minister prophetically to a woman who was on drugs and needed to hear and know that God still loved her and had not forgotten about her, although, she had rebelled against him for years. We also got a chance to minister to a young woman who had been on her own since the age of thirteen. That day she heard the word of the Lord and a change began to transpire in her life.

My husband and I got our new vehicle from God's chosen place and choice which became our choice after seeking God in prayer and turning over our own willful desire concerning the other truck. After we had left the car lot and God had blown our minds with a restoration of soul winning and lower miles on an exact vehicle, we had a peace that surpassed all understanding. We loved our new SUV and it speaks the heart of God. Our daughters loved it as well. After all the tight car rides they had better. Isn't it like God to sometimes humble you while yet in a tight place, hoping and believing for Him to bring you out into a larger plane or territory? Accepting God's will is the perfect key to drive with.

Another testimony in accepting God's plan is when I got pregnant with my daughter. I thought I would not make it. My husband had to keep reminding me of God's word and help me push on a day to day basis. At that time I was the only one in my home working while my husband was going strong in full time ministry for five years. About this time the economy had just gone into a major recession and people had stopped giving to the ministry because of fear, being afraid of what would happen if they had sacrificed giving and what effect it would have on them. I say it was just not willing to totally walk by faith and readjust something to live a sold out life for God through Christ. As my husband encouraged me through our pregnancy, I encouraged him to stay focused on God and to not get a job. He went looking and people were calling.

But, after hearing God say He was our supplier, I told my husband let's just keep it moving and trust God. I did not want any trouble at that point with God or man with the way I had been feeling in this pregnancy. At the time before coming into full time ministry with my husband, I was a successful entrepreneur, a certified nursing assistant, working at a health and rehabilitation facility, in which I had to run the floor all eight hours of my shift pulling and lifting dead weight of the young and old patients.

I had to have the ambulance come to my job to rush me to the hospital as I was going into early term labor. It was terrible only to arrive at the hospital and then be sent home the same night. Although my husband was tired and, I could tell, frustrated having to deal with me and our three girls at the same time who were always talking to him about everything and loved to have his attention, just like their mommy. I could only imagine how he had to feel, trying to build the church, minister at the jail, taking the girls to school, doing their hair, watching carefully over me, cooking and cleaning, yet staying focused and determined. To see him willingly give me the courage to push and continue to go to work, even though sometimes I had to take off two and three days out of a pay period. I can remember my check being short and worrying how we were going to meet the bills. I tell you as I look back; I see it was nobody but God. I knew as a wife, mother and first lady, I had to allow God to get the glory out of my story.

At the end of my pregnancy in which I delivered three weeks early, I had suffered with placental abruption. I had to go and see my doctor for a checkup one morning and she told me that she could not hear our daughter breathing, so she wanted me to go straight to the hospital and get an ultrasound. Before I went to the hospital I drove home to pick up my husband. After arriving at the hospital and getting the test done, we were in for the news of our life. Our daughter was in my tummy as it was full of blood, her heart was beating but her breathing was gone. My husband and I were not in shock. Months earlier, my husband while we were lying in bed, turned to me and told me the Lord had said our pregnancy would be a miracle. And, I was like Lord, a miracle? What will happen next? SO when we heard about the blood in my belly and the baby not breathing, we looked at one another and knew it was the word God had spoken. I had to be taken in for emergency surgery. My husband and our three girls were there and saw the baby delivered.

That Sunday God also worked another miracle. Apparently even though I was doped up on medication, nurses and doctors say I had been ministering and prophesying to them about personal issues and they were amazed. My husband said he did not know of me doing any of this, but it proved to be correct. Our church was filled with the hospital staff that Sunday. Nurses and doctors arrived and they all were excited to be with us in the presence of the Lord. I came right out the hospital that Friday and went straight to church that Sunday. I sang a solo and did I sing my heart out so God would be glorified.

There was an anointing on my voice. After all my suffering for nine months, I birthed our baby. From all I was going through with being pregnant and having to have surgery, while yet standing against opposition with people who were throwing daggers and trying to block and stop my husband and I, I continued to stand and cheer.

Not in just word, but also in deed. I refused to leave my family hanging in a dry place. I can say it was truly worth it. I have seen so much growth in my family and in my life. I also see the blessings, not just in my daughter who is beautiful to behold, but I also see it in my ministry and the tangible assets God had blessed me with. Like every time I get in the driver's seat of the new Jaguar my husband bought me, I say thank you, Jesus. If my husband having compassion and seeing me go through all the pain I suffered, not just in carrying our child but in healing in all aspects, and, yet me being determined to push and birth his God given vision, call and destiny out of him, no matter the life I myself must sacrifice. Then let me suffer and continue to cheer. A muffled cheerleader is a weak cheerleader. But that one that stands and blows the trumpet and sounds the alarm will see the reward in her labor if she cheers and thanks God for the payoff later.

Being married, your mate's role is different from yours. Being one in marriage, your call, vision and plan should be the same and that is to stand and win the game while working, fasting and praying together. I have come across a lot of women in the church that are carnal minded. They want a husband to wash their feet, massage their back, pay every bill and scratch their head daily, yet never sending up a prayer for their mate, always expecting him not to say anything about any of the decisions made in the house. I have had to pray on occasion for women with such mindsets to understand that a man is God's before he is theirs and he must be free to answer God's call. These types of women are the ones that go to church on Easter Sunday and see how the men of God worship and praise God desiring for their husband to get saved and be like one of them while hoping that her one year visit to Mount Mariah Baptist will make a difference. Then, she comes home and starts treating her husband like an outcast forgetting it is he that pampers her. Most importantly, it is she that has failed to encourage herself to cheer him on by living a dedicated and devoted life unto God that would cause her husband to get saved and want to run for the Lord and catch the vision of the Kingdom of God.

I, as a leader, co-pastor, and first lady understand it is my job to pray for my husband daily, calling favor and doors to open for him to prosper; so, we as a unit may prosper as one while yet asking God to give him wisdom, balance and a little strength. So when he gets off the road from a busy schedule or working ministry, he would have a little strength when he gets home so that we can find one another, because the truth is we are soul mates, God given to one another. On a day to day basis, we have to find one another from the rush of a day to ushering one another back into the Garden of God's love by prayer, words of love, and, sometimes, just quiet peace and being still while resting and meditating on the goodness of our God while holding one another, enjoying one another and our love for one another and His love for us!

I am his cheerleader, his confidant, prayer partner, destiny keeper, b. f. f., and image of God when he needs to see a light in the midst of his darkest hours. I am the joy he sees in the morning, after the weeping in some midnight hours. I am his strength and helpmate. I am the one God sent to mend his broken heart, to help encourage him to love again even though he had been scarred. I am the one God used to erase the tragedy and past pains. I am the one God sent for him to lay down his worries, fears, shame and pain. I stand firm and in assurance to birth my God-sent man of promise and destiny, birthing him into places, both unreachable and distinct. God had given him to me off His pottered shelf and has entrusted me to call his life from a tomb of darkness praying that he be kept from the path of death.

I am a part of his bridges over troubled water, encouraging him daily to tread. I am his cheerleader, sent by God to help him hit a home run, score a touchdown, shoot in the hoops, all the while helping him stay focused.

Even though odds or darkness come against him or us, I will stand and continue to cheer for God's man to help him not fall but to stand tall. I am a woman of God, seasoned to cheer and be his cheerleader through the good, the bad, the ugly and all! Go; Go, Go he is my God given G.I. Joe!

This is the spirit, mind, and attitude for women to have for their diamond and pearl with sincere love, passion and compassion for the one God has given or will give her to cheer for and cheer with. I know because I live it and it is in me through prayer and obedience to the voice of God and His leading by the Holy Spirit!

Love,

Pastor Felicia S Cunningham
www.fscministries.com

Losing All Innocence

In this troubled world of affliction, burdens and scrutiny there are women hurting, bleeding on the inside. In our world today, these women attend church every Sunday, singing, praying, speaking in tongues and praising God from the depths of their broken hearts. It becomes harder and harder each week as they come to Sunday service, hoping to be heard by God to send them the man of their dreams because they think that he would be the answer they need.

They believe that he would fulfill the empty dark void of the past in becoming the father they never knew or maybe once had as a child, but then stolen by life and its rush of sin. She always dreamed of being Daddy's little girl. She is hoping he'd come as Daddy did when he surprised her with her first new Easter dress, smiling from ear to ear, as she ran and embraced him. This was her form of a thank you as she felt the warmth in her spirit and deep passion in her soul, feeling protected like the Queen in Buckingham Palace, while wrapped in his arms and feeling guarded by her Daddy's love, before losing all innocence.

She had hoped to receive that someone who would accept her for where she had been, but most of all for what she had experienced. She was hoping for someone that's not like all the other men she had encountered as a child and teen growing up, abandoned by her Father at five, raped at thirteen by a loved one and then by the most popular guy on the football team at school after inviting him over while her Mother was away.

Now she lives torn and empty in the pit of silence and in fear of telling anyone. Because of the shame and embarrassment she dreads to walk through as she ponders in her mind her own self-worthlessness and of being useless, blaming herself for all the abuses and terrible tragedies in her life. She is running and has run from her past in all aspects, drinking, drugging and the rage within while being greedy for money. She is struggling to keep up with the latest hairstyle, clothing, jewelry, purse, shoes, and make up as she tries to fill the emptiness in her dark soul and broken spirit.

She is willing to sell her most prized possession, as long as she doesn't have to face the past hurt and darkness of abandonment by her hero, Dad, and those terrible days and nights in her bedroom with the men who took what her Mother had told her to value most. She goes to school the next day with a smile outside, but a pain and discomfort within, wondering if anyone could truly read her thoughts or see her inner being as to what had happened six hours prior, before arriving at school.

While her mother slept from drinking and/or if she was sometimes away, her mother's boyfriend would slip away, entering her bedroom. He would draw near to where she lay, as she pretended to sleep, and he would begin to rub her legs while she shivered. Opening her mouth telling him to stop and saying no; but, yet, he continued, placing his hand over her mouth. He then proceeds to get on top, prowling her legs open with the weight of his body, then pulling aside her panties, penetrating and tarring her vagina. He, in turn, leaves her with a broken heart and a wounded spirit with tears rolling down her ruddy red cheeks and the blood consistently flowing that was stolen from her youth. Now, she carries her past in memories of darkness, with no hope, no future, dressing to entice the innocent men who will pay for the damage of her broken heart and shattered spirit.

As quoted by William Congreve, "Heaven has no rage like love to hatred turned, Nor hell a fury like a woman scorned."

In the Bible we find that there were all kinds of women that had issues or that had dealt with something tragic. They indeed had to face them, whether the issue or tragedy was caused by their own error or by someone else; or, if it was just plain life that threw a curve ball unknowingly, in which things in life happen. From the beginning of creation till now women have been attacked by the enemy and have had to suffer dreadful experiences that at some point moved them to cover them up with a made up spirit and mentality; thus, living in falsified beauty. At some point in their life, this causes them to grow deadlier and deader inside each day.

I have read a series of stories in the Bible and have experienced as a traveling Prophet/Evangelist around the United States to becoming a founder and Senior Pastor of three churches, the reenactment of women in the Bible played out through the lives of many women of today. Some have the same tragedy but different endings. Just like the fairy tales of our childhood. Believe it or not, these fairy tale stories are to prepare us for some sort of trial or crisis once we are older and to let us know that there is always hope at the end of each rainbow. Beauty had a beast which she fell in love with but had to wait for the change to come. She believed this would take place in time to her prince turning from a raging beast inwardly and outwardly to a handsome, sweet man all around. I'm talking about the women who are married and believe God for the salvation of their mate changing and turning their ugly attitude from being the worst to the best.

Cinderella stayed faithful through all the abuse that she received from her siblings. She was left to clean while her stepmother and step-sisters went to a ball to find a man.

In which, she ended up with one and not just anyone, but a Prince after her cry was heard by her fairy God-Mother. Her fairy God-Mother came and zapped her with a magic wand turning her from rags to riches, then sending her to the ball with instructions that she had to come back home before twelve or she would be found in rags by her prince. With Cinderella losing her shoe at the ball while trying to beat time really worked for her good. She was found in rags by her now husband for years. Ha, Ha! Mr. Prince found her at home while cleaning as her stepmother and step-sisters tried to hide her in the back dungeon. But, it didn't work because she was found by her man and then happily married.

This story is for all the women who feel that they have been put on the back burner. It seems like your family members have gotten married and your friends, and don't leave your haters and enemies out who have, and you are happy for them. But, when you talk about your dream man coming to and for you, they don't seem to be happy for you. They act as if they want you to stay as a cleanup woman covering and cleaning their messes. No, I am not talking about the 'Clean Up Woman' my Sister R/B Legend Betty Wright sings about. But, you be encouraged because the first shall be last and the last shall be first.

James 4:10 (WEB) states, *"Humble yourselves in the sight of the Lord and He will exalt (promote) you."*

1 Peter 5:6 (KJV) states, *"Humble yourselves therefore under the mighty hand of God, that he may exalt you in due time:"*

Snow White got tricked by her enemy to eat an apple that poisoned her, putting her to sleep until she was found and kissed by a charming prince. In which she awakened and lived happily ever after. This story is for all the women who trusted a friend or relative and then they stole your prince. They won't keep him. I know you were blinded as the witch came to your door, camouflaged as a snake, jealous and unhappy because she doesn't have your drive or charisma. The day before church, she gives you a gift certificate to go to the spa to get a good back massage. She knew that you were going to need it after you came home to find her in your bed with your husband, after seducing him with her shiny red apple.

Fairies were invited as Godmothers to the christening of the long wished for Princess. These Godmother Fairies offered gifts, such as beauty, wit, and musical talent to Sleeping Beauty. However, a wicked fairy that had been overlooked placed the Princess under an enchantment as her gift, saying that, on reaching adulthood, she would prick her finger on a spindle and die. A good fairy, though unable to completely reverse the spell, said that the Princess would instead sleep for a hundred years, until awakened by the kiss of a Prince. This Princess may have fallen asleep in her bed of sorrows. It may have seemed like it was all she wrote and that there would be no tomorrow, but her Prince Charming came along at the end, making his way through the thrones and thistles. Seeing her beauty, he kissed her and she woke up from her death match.

This story is for the women who are professional and business-minded who God is raising up to run His kingdom. Just because the sister in church who has been there for over twenty years did not get front row in your wedding or wasn't invited to your home so she might get up close and personal with you, hoping to manipulate you and your status. Now, she wants to speak death over you, saying all you will do will fail because they are the District Mother of whatever denomination you belong to. God doesn't see titles. He sure didn't see Jezebel's title, even though she was King Ahab's wife or Miriam's title when she spoke against Moses.

In each story we can see that it may have started out rough but the ending was beautiful. Like the fairy tales, God never ends the story without bringing back the glory, His glory.

When you look at each of these stories, each woman had someone hating them or who was jealous of them because of what they saw in them. The victims in these fairy tales couldn't see who they were or what gifts, talents or abilities they possessed but their enemy could. That's why they were targeted and fell into the traps of the enemy. They were gullible and fell for the bait.

If you noticed, all of these women walked alone and flowed with nature. You can't just go with anything and anybody. These women sang with the birds, danced with the deer, feed the rabbits or did something of such course before they found out that someone had their eyes on them, as they thought they were walking alone.

Jesus flowed with God's will, but He was discerning and knew who His enemy was.

I believe, just like these women, women of reality have to have had something happen to them for purpose and destiny to awaken in them. This caused them to be on guard for the drifts and crucial winds of life. As you can see in the end, they got blessed. They didn't allow their being victimized by the blows of life to stop their flow of love and to end their happiness. Once their eyes had opened from the sting of death, they received all that God had for them. They became perfected in time after being tested and becoming ready to walk with the one that He ordained to find them. At the end of each story, each victim had a Prince to rescue her.

Now, I know most women like this part but I want to explain something. Yes, these were men but not ordinary men. That is why they had to receive a Prince, one whom was charming, thoughtful, patient, giving, supportive, encouraging, understanding and loving. Someone sent by a King for purpose and destiny, holding power to not only change a life but to give life and that stood for righteousness with credit and credential behind His name.

Yes, Jesus is this Prince. Sent by the king, who gave His life for you, who willingly received you in the state and condition you were in when you were found broken, wounded, bitter, sick, blind and lame from whatever reason.

Now, it is up to you to get God in your life totally so you can be healed and set free, drawing your husband's attention to the beauty of holiness in you. So that when he comes and sees you, even if you are in a wilderness experience he will see the heart of Ruth in you, a willingness, a drive, a persistence, perseverance, compassion, love and by far, the most important, a woman who is committed to and after the heart of God. A Prince knows his Princess once he sees her.

For the word of God declares in **Proverbs 18:22 (NASB)** *"He who finds a wife finds a good thing And obtains favor from the Lord."*

Now this scripture is not talking about a woman who wants a man who is trying to show herself approved by God by attending church every Sunday or who is in every Bible study class or conference meeting. No, this woman is already committed to the Lord in all her ways and has nothing to prove because she understands as long as God heals her troubled heart and delivers her bitter spirit, even if she doesn't receive the man she has dreamed of, she knows as long as she has King Jesus she doesn't need anybody else. Her focus is to seek and please God; that is why the Bible says "he who finds a wife."

Wife means a woman of commitment. She is already married to God. She has her void filled and her cup running over with God giving into her bosom that is why she does not need any jigalow to fill it. She is never caught off guard and doesn't have time to worry about if a man will come, keeping her life on hold before she makes up her mind to move forward with her God given dreams and destiny. She already has learned to rest in God and knows He has her best interest at heart. Her focus and purpose is to live before God so that when her husband finds her, he won't find the little girl who was hurt and abused as a child coming up, making him pay unknowingly for what has happened to her in the past by all the other men who had taken advantage of her on those dark lonely nights.

Proverbs 14:1 (NRSV) declares, *"The wise woman builds her house, but the foolish tears it down with her own hands."*

A woman can tear down with her hands that which God is trying to build using her for the establishment. She does this by nagging her mate about things only God can change, having outbursts of wrath, and acting in uncivilized manners because of an unhealed heart while experiencing frustrations with an inner rage within her spirit man, throwing temper tantrums. She feels that the man God has now sent her is not accommodating her in the right way. By not taking time to examine herself, she doesn't realize that it is really her not finding happiness within herself because she failed to steal away and get down on her knees seeking God for her healing and deliverance while consistently preparing for her date with destiny and promise of life. So when he arrived she would have a heart of gold and a sweet spirit that only God could measure.

If a woman doesn't take time out to exercise her ability to communicate with God, then she will fail in communicating with her husband or any other person at that. She will push him or those away into a place of silence due to her uncontrollable emotions that only God can tame. How can a Prince rule a portion of the King's house if he is being knock off focus by the supposed to be Princess, who has all these past and present issues that are causing her not to excel spiritually and mentally but rather decline? This causes even those around her to decline.

Women who are after God's heart know that if they do not get God in their spirit, their soul, their mind and their heart by entering His presence daily, they will die without seeing God's promises fulfilled in their lives. They will continue to walk in misery killing everyone and everything spiritually and, in some cases, physically because of the death that lingers in their mind and spirit. Women out of sorts will never have anything nice to say. They will always be negative, seeing negativity in every situation. She will never be able to associate with others on a one on one basis without having to feel she needs to be in control. She will feel as if she has to fight her way through life doing whatever it takes, not regarding her associates or affiliates along life's way. She believes that by keeping her walls up, it shows her strength as she wrestles and fights with childhood and adult memories of the past hurts she incurred those terrible nights and days she was victimized. So she steals away from people and keeps to herself as she did in Junior High, after becoming a victim to her loved ones. She is hoping that no one can see her past secrets. Not wanting to slip up and breakdown from showing herself to be strong in front of the crowd at work or at church, all the while telling herself that God is all I need. She does not know that people want to reach out and be her friend. Many are in fear of drawing near even to say 'hello' thinking they may fall into her valley of dread and uncertain death because of those brutal eyes and the mean look on her face. They do not know or realize how much she is hurting within as she keeps up the pretenses for others to see.

Proverbs 18:24 (KJV), *"A man that has friends must show himself friendly: and there is a friend that sticks closer than a brother."*

Tragedies as Boys Affected as Men

In this world of sin and darkness, yet, called to walk and to fulfill righteousness through a committed relationship with God through His Son and Sacrifice, Jesus Christ, Lord and Savior, there remains hurt, bitterness, theft, deceit, unforgiveness, judging, hatred, killing and coveting, just to name a few of life's dark halos. In the midst of this pollution there are men pondering in the thoughts of their minds how life would have been better if their father had been around to give them guidance and protection as they grew to mature from a boy to a man.

Hiding what had happened to him as a child, tortured by his past, wrestling with childhood memories and inner thoughts of the abuse and molestation from the man he was looking to be his Father in his life, but now, he is haunted by that face. The love and respect that he had for the one he sighted as Daddy and verbally called Freddy was taken for granted. The same one whom he needed to teach him how to stand against the giants that would try to abort his destiny as he was growing up from a boy to a Godly man in this imperfect world of sin.

Both of his parents, his occasional responsible Mom and should have been hero Dad, were stolen by the lust of the eye and the pride of life with both lacking the knowledge as a man and woman to stand in the world seeking God's eternal plan for their son. Because of the tragedy as a child, their son now stands alone in a deep dark place tortured mentally and spiritually, confused with mixed emotions as to whether to marry a woman or live a secretive life liking men.

While growing up he remembered how he had once tried to prove himself to friends, wanting to get rid of the battle within by doing everything possible to fit in with his guy friends, hoping that would change some of his feminine ways of thinking and emotions. Running from his past has affected his future. Feeling isolated in the crowd as his friends mentioned while walking by some distinguished educated young man on the way to the ball court, "Look at home boy, he's a gay." He too is trying to hide the wounds of being victimized.

Now, he is hanging out with the guys in the club. Not knowing that some of them have experienced even greater torment as they once laid naked in a dark room while their most trusted loved one and supposed to have been substitute super hero has them thinking night after night "why me." They were made to become something opposite of their male DNA, forced to do things they were never born to do orally and sexually as they are told to be silent. With their mouth muffled and while in pain, they are penetrated; thus, losing their manhood and all their self-confidence, yet receiving the deposit and seed of defiled demonic sexual spirits that their molester incurred in the same manner the night he was taken advantage of when he was being victimized at a tender young age.

Now with no control, walking with a treacherous curse, wondering day after day what would be the response if they told a soul. But most important, what would happen if their football buddies on the team at school found out. They were in a constant spiritual battle that tormented them mentally and spiritually. They had to take showers with their teammates in the guys' locker room after practice or a game, off the ball field. They were trying not to glance at their fellow teammates as they washed the sweat off their athletic muscular bodies while battling the lust of the eye.

Now grown, all of them are playing hard with their outer appearance. Deep on their inside there is a cry for help, needing to tell someone, hoping for help and a cure to stop feeling the urge that dwells in their spirit and mind. The truth is, now they desire something they didn't desire from an earlier age. Their flesh screams and races, lusting for the man in the club dancing with his girlfriend, hoping that they are not seen gazing at the way he moves while holding his companion tight in his arms. They ask themselves will he play, is he straight, fronting, bi or gay, as their flesh outrageously craves for this ungodly satisfaction.

Now there is another fight and disturbance as a lustful rage takes place for their childhood friend who has showed them much love, having been (boy) friends forever since the time of being little toddler boys. They are grown now and feeling emotions for one another within, as they have spent time with one another growing together, riding tricycles, shooting ball, playing video games, and wrestling one another. Fighting and saying no, no, I can't be thinking this way. I want to please God but this mental stage keeps getting me to disobey in thought and in heart. So he hurries up and departs, leaving his friend, so that the truth stays untold about the fight he is having in life, because he doesn't want to break that bridge of friendship. If his friend doesn't receive the truth of how he feels from his past to his present, wrestling with what most men would call unpleasant. As if it was a disease or an unforgivable sin that God cannot deliver them from or clean them from within, transforming the mind of the individual, thus, bringing them out of the pothole of darkness to the throne of rulership.

Then, there are Sundays, as they have gone and do go to attend service, hoping today will be their day of deliverance from feeling and thinking such ways. Their mind cannot seem to focus on the service due to the traditional church setting and atmosphere of stagnation and powerless teaching that God loves you where you are and for who you are. You are driven crazy mentally trying to stop thinking such thoughts in the house of faith while the brother in the Canali Designer Suit and Stacy Adams Designer Shoes is making his way up front to pay his tithe.

Not knowing whom to trust or whom to tell, afraid it may get out, abroad, among loved ones and close friends. Wanting to tell his fiancé, but will she still love him? Or will she leave him standing still at the altar, divorcing him before the marriage is signed and sealed? Maybe she will feel betrayed, overlooking trust, disregarding their love because of the rusted chains that he received that night while being raped by a kinsman, which has bound him mentally and has tried to possess him spiritually.

Feeling defeated and trapped. Alone. Not knowing what to do or who to lean on, not willing to trust anyone, thinking that they may be treated as they were in the past, by the man who took advantage of their trust the night he took their pride in those hours of brutal darkness…

Stories like this sound devastating, don't they? Well, they are true and have happened and are happening to someone right now, today. This is why if God's people desire to become set free from whatever state and issues of their past life and to be able to live free, moving forward in drive and no longer residing in neutral, they must start facing reality and stop hiding, taking no for an answer when God is the answer. I say it again, "Things of this nature have happened and are happening!" Whether it is in the USA, China, or Africa or in another country, the enemy and sin are loose in the world today, captivating many.

Thus, causing damage to many spiritually, physically, and mentally affecting them emotionally, leaving many with a bad taste of life as they live in dark tombs trapped by men in old grave clothing, believing and feeling that there is no hope for tomorrow.

I thank God, through Christ Jesus, that there is hope for all who are experiencing such a life of distraught. As the Lord called Lazarus in **John 11:44** from behind the tombs and commanded that the stone be rolled away, calling him from a sleep (dead) commanding that he be loosed from the stench of death and grave clothing, **so has He called you!** In life, things happen at an early age to many. At some point one begins to function disorderly and improperly, living confused and rigid lives, sitting and wondering why me. Always wondering, thus questioning themselves will their life ever turn around? Will my life go from being its worst to being healed, delivered and happy and not having to wrestle that I may live a life pleasing unto Father God? Will they be blessed by Him to have great prosperity and success as they have dreamed and envisioned, pretending to be a police officer, a fire fighter, or even the President of the United States? At their tender young ages while fresh as a flower on a spring day or like the freely flowing streams of crystal clear water in the Zephyrhills Bay, they dream, before life visits them with their bed time, boogie man.

I was praying during my normal hour of prayer each day from six (6) PM to seven (7) PM, when I heard the Lord say, "I want you to write a book entitled "Shattered Mirrors." I was excited about the title not knowing what it was going to be about or why he had told me to title it by name. I was excited because I knew if God said to do so, then this project would be in season with Him and His divine will, bringing deliverance and healing to the spirit, the soul, the heart, and the mind of the chained and bound.

I had just started working on another piece of literature a few days earlier, after the Lord had released me to write again, but I put it off for months. Actually, I had put off writing again for two or three years since I had gone through so much warfare after my first book was released in 2007, (details will be in "Broken for Such 2", coming soon), while waiting on the Word of the Lord through prayer and fasting. Though I had the title and words of knowledge to speak on the issue of the other project, it is just like God to interrupt your plans and give you His orders.

Proverbs 16:9 (AKJV) declares, *"A man's heart devised his way: But the Lord directs his steps."*

I then asked God what He would have me to write about, since He had given me the title, but no information on what the title was about.

I was clueless. After trying to figure it out in my mind and receiving no answer, I did what we are created to do. I went to my former living room area in my home and I worshiped the Lord for hours until He lead me into the Spirit realm and showed me what was happening to boys who have become malfunctioned men and girls who have become malfunctioned women. As I was in the Spirit, the Lord spoke saying, "This book will not only be a book of knowledge but of My Spirit as I take you into the deeper depths of My heart to see the sin and feel the infirmities of My people whom I have called in this present age. You are going to write about things that many are running from and some leaders, pastors and preachers are scared to address and deal with; from hurt, abuse, misuse, and the stench of death while dwelling in the tombs. Many are cutting themselves inwardly with broken, sharp ended mirrors.

Let's go to **Luke 8:26-39 (NKJV),**

A Demon Possessed Man Healed

Luke 8:26-27 *"Then they sailed to the country of the Gadarenes, which is opposite Galilee. And when he stepped out on the land, there met him a certain man from the city who had demons for a long time. And he wore no* *clothes, nor did he live in a house, but in the tombs."*

When you read these two verses you find that when Jesus arrived on the scene, he meets a man with demons, very strong demons at that. The Bible also speaks of the man not wearing any clothing nor living in a house, but that he dwelt in tombs. In order for this man to have gotten into this predicament, one would say something had to have happened to him that caused him to shut down, driving him into a place of darkness, sin and death where the enemy, Satan, dwells.

The Bible doesn't state what happened to him but the Bible shows us he was not stable. His spirit was tainted and he dwelt in a mindset of death, tombs.

The definition of tombs is a dead place of memory or memories of one or many things that have occurred. That memory is deep inside that one who is afflicted and who goes and lives or has lived spiritually and mentally causing life to be chained, bitter and neutral.

The memories are so deeply embedded inside his heart, mind, soul, and spirit creating spiritual and mental anguish; thus, causing bitterness and a chained neutral life.

In other words, he allowed what had happened to him in the past from his loved ones or possibly his self-wrong to manipulate and control his future. He wanted to forgive others, but could not. He wanted to forgive himself, but did not know how. He wanted to stop thinking about what had happened to him long ago but was bound. He had no knowledge of the power of God to release the darkness from his mind and spirit.

As I was born a Prophet to the Nations and given an the Apostolic mantle by the Lord of lords and King of kings, working with men of all ethnic and backgrounds, I have learned to know that body language plays a major role in our everyday lives.

We in the kingdom of God call it a gift of discernment as in **1 Corinthians 12:10**, a gift that is God given.

Not to think someone or something may be, but to really know they are. It is because of God's leading, hearing His voice with our spiritual eyes and ears being opened, so life will come forth when we speak.

When you read that this man wore no clothing, you find that this is a sign of wanting to be free, yet having no discipline. He makes a statement outwardly with his carnal nature by the removal of his clothing, which symbolizes entrapment and the weight of one internally. Even Satan desires to be free and to have all power and authority to do as he pleases, with no self-control or limitation, just like this man. As being a Pastor for eight years, some of my members and believers of Christ have come and asked on occasions, why is it that their two year old son or daughter likes taking off his or her clothing, and not wanting to wear a diaper at such a young age. Through the unction of the Holy Spirit, God began to reveal to me that this is a sign of wanting to be free. Most of the time when a child is learning something new, especially potty training, the child feels as if it is better to be without clothing; thus, showing a form of rebellion. Or, it could be the child's way of struggling physically and dealing mentally with the challenge of learning something new that will improve his life.

The Bible states that the man did not live in a house which symbolizes two views. The man had no order or way of living, focusing on the past and dwelling in the tombs, which caused him to miss the things he needed to learn and experience to be able to cope with others to broaden his future. The past storms of a negative life and the experiences of brutal pain have paralyzed him spiritually and mentally causing him to be a walking corpse, thus, a stagnate human being. Instead of taking the past and using it as a growing lesson for the future, he held on to that which may have wronged him but could have truly blessed Him.

We must also consider him not wanting to be boxed in, feeling bound and suffocated, battling the warfare of freedom mentally, not wanting to look at himself and face past tragedies and devastation from either family, friends or associates. Speaking of past events or, rather, be it that he would have to meditate on some things he did not want to face because he had not yet learned of grace and forgiveness. Unable to find a positive answer for his ill state brings him to a dormant place of having no integrity or character for himself or life, as he runs loose in his inner thoughts. The book of James defines it as being double minded, which means not on a solid foundation, and unstable.

James 1: 8 (KJV) *"A double minded man is unstable in all his ways."*

The afflictions from his past caused him to lose all self-control allowing bitter seeds to become demonic spirits that settled within his soul and spirit, tormenting him mentally driving him into a wild place.

In this story, the wilderness or a wild place is perceived as a dangerous force that confounds order, bringing pursuits of human culture and agriculture. Wilderness, according to this story, is cognate with wastefulness. Wild places resist conversion to human use; therefore, they must be destroyed or overcome.

Luke 8:28 (NKJV), *"When he saw Jesus, He cried out, fell down before him, and with a loud voice said, "What have I to do with You, Jesus, Son of the Most High God? I beg you, do not torment me!"*

Now when you look at this verse you begin to see this demon possessed man, the one who had been afflicted for a long time, seeing Jesus coming, in the no help for him days when every man has given up on him. He sees Jesus from afar and he cries aloud, falling down into a worship mode, representing a sign of unworthiness, shame, tiredness and submissiveness, asking what have I to do with you?... Now, here is a man needing help, healing and deliverance asking the Lord and Savior, who has the power to change a life, which is the light and who has taken authority over darkness, what have I to do with you, when needing to be set free!

It baffled me. What would make this man say such a thing? Was it the demonic spirit speaking at the time, trying to stop the deliverance of the man? Was it because the man had come to the point of feeling unworthy of his deliverance due to the way he had been treated by others in his past? These same ones may have given up on him and said that he deserved to be in his tormented state for the spiritual illness he had inherited as there was no power from the pulpit to denounce, bind or loose it.

After viewing this paragraph, I imagined there had to be a time when this man did not want to hurt anyone or react in harshness. But because of the adopted anger and rage he felt rising within himself, knowing that he would be capable of tearing down, destroying others emotionally, he searched for help. Instead of receiving the help that he so desperately wanted and needed, he became worse. Every bridge that had been built to help him live a successful life was destroyed because of the breech within his heart and soul.

Jesus arrived when the demon possessed man was all alone and left for dead in a wild place, the wilderness, dwelling next to swine. Kinda like the prodigal son who chose to take his inheritance and live a foolish lifestyle, living for the moment satisfying only himself. He was trying to buy friendship, no matter the cost. After all his inheritance had been spent living this life of pleasure with others, he was cast out. He wound up taking care of the pigs.

This is how the secular world works. It invites you in, but you better be coming with something valuable in your hand. It doesn't tell you to bring wisdom, understanding or common sense with you. So when you are broke with no resources and you do not have a plan or vision for your life, for your future on how to push the twelve systems of the world to function, you are a cast out, thrown away.

But just like God, through His infinite mercy, He comes when we are forsaken and our backs are up against the wall with nobody to talk to, nobody to lean on and our shape or condition has escalated to its full capacity of no hope.

Talking about a near death experience, hitting the bottom of the pit where one suffers loss, then redemption is fulfilled through Christ

Jesus, because of the recognition of one's state of being and then the anointed one, Jesus, which is the main key after one falls into serenity and worships the Lord for DELIVERANCE and FREEDOM.

Luke 8:29 (NKJV) *"For He had commanded the unclean spirit to come out of the man. For it had often seized him, and he was kept under guard, bound with chains and shackles; and he broke the bonds and was driven by the demon into the wilderness."*

Luke 8:29b (NKJV) states that the man *"was kept under guard, bound with chains and shackles; and he broke the bonds driven by the demons into the wilderness."*

In times of such matters, when a person is already in a crisis they don't need any more spiritual or mental weight. This man was kept under guard meaning there was someone watching over him in his condition. They were not able to get to the root of the problem that would set him free or help him to become free. They were only adding more weight and bondage to his inner and physical being with chains that were broken and shackles that were busted loose. (The chains that are broken represent relationships, meaning links, associations, or connections to others.

The shackles that are burst represent man's temporary fixer upper, meaning their own psychological system and rituals that do not prevail.)

This is what people who are broken and bound themselves do, who don't know Christ, the Redeemer, and have not experienced His full power and wholeness through a relationship with the Father. They are operating in a state of man's intellect, having word recognition but having no word comprehension and having no obedience to experience the power of God through the gospel. They cannot bring deliverance to its full capacity by the Spirit of God and the knowledge of His Kingdom themselves since they themselves haven't been delivered or experienced deliverance and freedom in Christ. In other words, they are self-made, home-made, giving themselves a title and name, such as, an Apostle, a Prophet, an Evangelist, a Pastor, a Teacher, but have not experienced the resurrection and power of Jesus Christ. Nor have they been called by Him and Him alone. They may be operating off a gift or a talent and are confused that their gift is not the anointing or presence of God!

Romans 11:29 (KJV Online) *"For the gifts and calling of God [are] without repentance."*

Matthew 22:14 (KJV) declares *"Many are called but few are chosen!"*

Have you ever been to the emergency room, at night in the midnight hours? After waiting patiently for your name to be called while suffering in excruciating pain, you had to first sign in, then you had to have your vitals taken, along with having blood pressure tests done before you could see the doctor. After waiting a little longer, you are taken back to a room and according to your problem, you may or may not be asked to strip naked and to put on a thin gown that has no covering in the back.

Finally, the doctor in charge of the ER (emergency room) comes to your room, introducing his/her self, asking you where you are hurting. After answering the doctor's questions, you are examined by the doctor using their hands to find out where the pain resides and to see if there is more pain that you are not aware of that may be affecting you which is consistent to the pain that you are already experiencing. You are then asked for your family history. Does your Father or Mother have high blood pressure, sugar diabetes, cancer and such?

If it is your head that has been injured, they ask, "Did you fall and bump your head?" If it's your leg or arm, they ask you if you think it is broken or sprained. If it is internally, they ask where the pain is. Then, they check you for any internal bleeding by asking you to take a urine test. Shortly, thereafter, you are rolled away for a scan and/or an x-ray to be done on the area that you have inquired about. Well, imagine that your head was hurting and your heart was aching with flares that you couldn't describe, not knowing you were getting ready to find out that you have taken upon an illness that has affected your family linage, such as, heart failure, diabetes, or such.

You have overheard one of the nurses speaking about the newbie doctor and the fact that he/she has very little experience, if any, in the field of practice that you came in for treatment at the ER. You further find out that this temporary doctor has been released into the medical field for about two years now. I know, you definitely wouldn't want this doctor sending you home with instructions to take Tylenol after suffering a while from the painful illness that you are experiencing.

Now that you have come to find that this MD lacks experience as a doctor who deals with issues at hand on a daily basis like yours, you are rushed out into the discharge area. The day has been long and the hospital is short staffed, but the doctor releases you in your ill condition. The doctor has been rushing patients off without proper treatment due to him or her being tired, sleepy and frustrated, wrestling with mental matters themselves of the pending divorce they are facing at home and their child being on marijuana, lacking in school and/or making bad grades.

The doctor does not give any patients a referral to a physician that is an expert in handling the pain issues that you are being tormented with at this time. He or she is hoping Tylenol will get you through your pain and misdiagnosis of heartburn and lack of sleep, while your life is on the line and you are just moments away from a heart attack and brain aneurism.

Well, think about how it would feel to be kept under guard by a man who could care less about you and your problems, seeing you and your condition as a money market making a day's living off of you. For the most part, not wanting or trying to find or refer you to the help you need concerning your situation or problem. Imagine them chaining you, committing you, to man-made stipulations and misdiagnosis. Then, they are telling you that if you don't allow them to treat you with hard iron (weight) mentally, you won't be free. Thus, bounding you with conditions that they can't fulfill and that have not worked in the past for them.

The worst people to associate with are the ones who bring problems but never have a solution to them, when the solution is sometimes as simple as ABC, 123. These types of people can tell you that you are wrong all day long and pick and poke at the problem or even you. You never hear them say anything positive that will give hope for healing or belief for deliverance. It is kinda like having a parent who tells a child that they are in need of a haircut but they never put forth an effort into getting their child to the barber shop.   They complain each morning, sometimes weeks in advance about the child's hair being too long, too thick, too bushy, or too nappy. In some cases, they tell their child not to smoke weed or crack, but they are firing up the pipe or stem every chance they get while trying to run away from their past hurts, present stress, and insecurities. The solution is to lead by example by facing the reality of asking God for help on the earth concerning life and situations that seem unbearable.

Joel 2:32 (NASB) *"And it will come about, that whoever calls on the name of the LORD Will be delivered;"*

In my first book, "Broken for Such", I talk about my prison experience and how most of the officers were disrespectful to the inmates for no apparent reason. I also spoke about how the Department of Corrections pushed change according to man's tradition and personal intellect. Some of the officers needed a change and an attitude adjustment badly as they themselves had not experienced true change nor did they believe in or care for it personally. Most officers worked for state benefits and a check to be able to get free living in the state's trailer park while barely making a living on their J.O.B. meaning 'Just over Broke'.

I also noticed while I was incarcerated, the system or government says incarceration is to rehabilitate you, but how could this be? There is no love or concern there. The system is built on making money, enforcing daily routine without strategies for the inmates to prosper or to accomplish success after being released back into society with convicted records and with revoked civil rights.

By placing someone who has experienced a life of abuse, neglect, and wrongful acts all their childhood and adult life in this type of system with bounds and chains around people with the same issues will only create more issues for them. Why? A crook, liar, thief, burglar, etc. is only going to talk about what they have done or experienced. They exchange information on how to commit another crime without getting caught. They meditate on what they did and how they can prevent getting caught the next time by doing what they did but at a greater capacity.

Then there are some who dream of going to college to change their lives but those dreams are stolen from them because of the surrounding negative influences, attitudes and spirits of others. Then there are those who speak negativity consistently in the state's corrections system from the officers to the inmates which causes their minds to stay stagnate and their spirits to be bottled. Meanwhile, they are carrying spiritual stillborn babies that have been choked by the umbilical cord of bitterness because they have never been able to fulfill their dreams or see their visions come to pass for their future.

Not realizing that their past errors will be used by God for their present success to life. Since the past way of doing wrong has become like a spiritual and mental disease to them, similar to the DC numbers worn daily while incarcerated, thus remaining in the computer system worldwide. Once released back into the streets while applying for a career or a local job, that serial number will be a constant reminder to them of where they have been and the crimes they have committed; thus, blinding them from a new life. The wrestle of being productive in life has become their focus above everything else.

I have found from the jail house to the White House that no man or woman who works on the grounds from the warden to the officer in the guard tower to the garden keeper is able to proclaim liberty in Christ or whatever they believe to be true. This is because of the state's rule of no religion or faith sharing beliefs being allowed on the grounds. Some of them are still wrestling with past issues from their childhood, like the bedtime boogie man, who has come to get revenge on innocent blood, who did a crime, but wasn't there the night when their bedroom light was turned off. Caspar wasn't such a friendly ghost!

Feeding a person and telling them when to go to sleep and when to arise is not rehabilitation. If you don't get to the root of the problem by bringing the only true solution which is Christ, the problem will never cease. You can't tame a human as you tame a wild animal. Sometimes even lions and bears that have been tamed turn and bite the hand that feeds them.

God is the only source for a person's freedom.

He is the only one that can draw a person to Himself expecting change and He is able to keep them committed to change. In the last days, some of the same men who tell you to lock your doors for your protection will be the same ones breaking in it because they do not have a relationship with or freedom in Christ. You may wonder, why? While God's will abounds, man's system fails all the time.

Psalms 127:1-2 *"Unless God builds the house (mind, body, souls, spirit) they that build it labor in vain..."*

Many Christians and curious secular individuals have asked how I went through the prison system and managed to prosper and become successful in all that I have accomplished and done, and how it is that I am still standing. I simply state that I never lost my obedience to the voice of God. Although I have made errors in my walk with God as an immature saint or Christian and have delayed my process and growth in Him, I was always determined to get back up and back in line in my walk with Him through a heart of sincere repentance. Most of all, I never lost my love, my praise and my thanksgiving by giving God all the glory through my trials of life after my release.

This is what I did not have or knew of since years prior to me giving my life to the Lord before my date with darkness, wrong turns and prison experience. I was rebellious and had no spiritual order or discipline in Christ. That's why I am on earth in the world but not of the world. Thirteen years later preaching, singing, teaching and working miracles for God, our Father through Christ Jesus around the world, but most of all, my dedicated lifestyle of holiness and staying true of where I am in God and my love for the Lord and His people, to having a favored life with God and man.

They questioned me as to whether there ever was a time that I felt lost while incarcerated? I tell them it's just like the man who dwelt in the tombs. He had gotten to a point of being tired, and though possessed with demonic spirits as I was, he was tired of being driven in the wild. So, when Christ was reintroduced to me I fell down and worshiped Him and allowed Him to set me free and use me and my life testimonies and trials for Kingdom building purposes for His glory!

The thing is you never truly lose time. It is what you learn in and from it and what you do with it. In God there is no loss of time while you are able to breathe. He stated that He will use what was for the bad and make it for our good. If I had not been allowed to go to prison, I don't think I would have ever surrendered my life to the Lord as I did or received my God given call of Him choosing me. Life had gotten too much for me out in the world. As I came to the point in life of having no control, I was glad to finally cry out and lay down my will. I put myself in the enemy's hands allowing myself to be put to an open shame, falling flat on my face, but believe it or not, that is when wisdom kicks in. Most people have sense enough to surrender to the will of God.

I was tired of living in excuses and pretending to be something I was not. When you pretend to be something you are not, you open yourself up to all kinds of spirits. Like my grandmother used to say if you tell a lie, then you have to tell another and another to cover up each lie. Then you have to try and live them, not always knowing to whom you told what. I have learned you work harder to pretend than being for real with God and for real with yourself.

I have had some stumbling blocks and some stepping stones along the way. But, I am determined to allow God to use me and get the glory out of my life. I allowed the devil to use me for a season, but thanks to God, for Jesus Christ, I am here covered in the blood and refined like gold. Many people counted me out, thinking I would return to crime and do the same things I was doing; but He broke the chains, meaning God, in Christ Jesus!

Mark 6:4 (KJV) and **Matthew 13:57 (KJV)** state *"A prophet is not without honor but in his own country,"* meaning among his own people.

People who are usually in your past that were close to you at a period never want to acknowledge God in you. It is only because God has used you to show them up. Or possibly, they are too caught up on the person they saw born into life and growing up in front of them. They don't know how to take you or know how to bless God for you. Since they were actually the ones with their mouth on you in the first place, o, o. Let me get off this subject before I have some problems with some of my loved ones and pretending friends and associates who will read this book.

People don't like the truth nowadays, but I am going to tell it. Like I always say, "You don't have to talk about me, I'll talk about me and tell you whatever you want to know," and don't tell it for me. Let me tell it. You may add something to it or take away from it, so God won't get the glory for the story! That's right, move out of the way and I will tell it. Out of the confession of the demon possessed man, he was made whole and through my confession as well, I was and am wrong and God is right! That is how I managed to get delivered and set free and have managed to stay that way.

In my walk with God, I have had not just family, but friends and associates, who were highly gifted in the prophetic realm who were not clean spiritually and mentally. I found this to be so later. The ones whom the Lord had me walk with after my release from prison who tried to manipulate me. Even so much as going behind my back, trying to destroy my ministry and bind my success in God, because of their jealousy and disobedience to God in not answering the call of God for their own life.

Like one particular time years ago, the Lord had me to put a conference together which caused major exposure for the Kingdom and the Glory of God. When I was asked to do a radio interview and share with a radio personality the good news about what God had done for me through this door of opportunity that He had opened, they went to the talk show host to spread garbage about me, trying to stop the radio interview from happening. Instead of rejoicing that God would be glorified in this radio interview, envy and jealousy arose within causing them to spread untruths about how God had changed my life. But you know no weapon, devil! As a matter of fact this particular individual is stagnant to this day. He has had opportunities abroad in ministry, but because he had attempted to abort the ministry and destiny of great men and women of God, along with mine, he has seen very little, if any, manifestations of God or success while ministering abroad.

So, as you can see, I have walked through many trials, but I refused to allow myself or anyone to chain me again. The enemy will come to tempt and try you wanting to put you back into the same boat or have you turning your boat around or jumping overboard. But the power God has given man is greater than any power on the earth or in heaven, except for the power God alone possesses in His sovereign Kingdom!

The door is His Son, Jesus! If he brought you out, no man can send you back. If He stood you up, no man can sit you down. If He has freed you, then no man can chain you. In the past I have had the enemy even use people who I have fed, put roofs over their heads, and given clothing to lie about me trying to stop God's will from progressing in my life. But, what pastor or renown leader has not. We hear of the rumors, slandering, and setups almost every day through the news, Internet, and weekly magazines or newspapers!

As a pastor and a single father for a long period of time, I met some of the greatest people in God. I say in God, as God had given me the gift of discernment. In the Spirit, at times, I would see wonderfully gifted and beautiful individuals in Christ. I allowed myself to be blindsided (sighted) by spiritual sight instead of being aware of what was going on around me. Thus, allowing certain people in my circle of ministry and life without being precocious (cautious). After a season, some of these same individuals walked out of my life and ministry.

Others I dismissed as God told me to release them out of my life as He called and continues to call me to higher realms and dimensions in Him, leaving the old behind and pressing into the new. When God is trying to perfect that which concerns you and establish you in new thought patterns, behaviors and sensibility in Him and to life, you can't take everybody with you!

Psalms 138:7-8 (KJV), *"Though I walk in the midst of trouble, You will revive me; You will stretch out Your hand Against the wrath of my enemies, and Your right hand will save me. The Lord will perfect that which concerns me..."*

Acts 4:13 (NLT) describes what I'm testifying of well, *"The members of the council were amazed when they saw the boldness of Peter and John, for they could see that they were ordinary men with no special training in the Scriptures. They also recognized them as men who had been with Jesus."*

The enemy, Satan, is after the mind of a believer. If he can get the believer to believe the opposite of what God has spoken in His word concerning His children then he knows he can get the individual believer to abort their purpose, destiny and assignment from impacting and changing lives through the gospel of Jesus Christ. The enemy reminds us of our weak places in life, such as, can't speak, not educated enough, not pretty enough, not rich enough, didn't live yesterday with enough integrity. But God's Word tells us He has called us as a holy nation, a royal priesthood **(1 Peter 2:9**). God also loves to use the imperfections of our today to promote our tomorrow.

Jeremiah 29:11 *"For I know the thoughts that I think toward you, Says the LORD, thoughts of peace, and not of evil, to give you a hope and a future to bring you to an expected end."*

He is the potter we are the clay. In the justice system of men, which was built by the law of God yet given over to the power of Satan, we find a man is condemned or judged by his own mouth or past actions. But, in God we are redeemed from our past failures and polished in His presence toward glory to glory.

For the word of the Lord declares in **Matthew 12:43-45 (NCV)** *"When an evil spirit comes out of a person, it travels through dry places, (Jesus said, out of your belly will flow rivers of living water, where there is not the Holy Spirit the enemy is able to possess that building) looking for a place to rest. But when it finds no place, it says, 'I will go back to the house I left.' And when it comes back, it finds that house swept clean and made neat. Then the evil spirit goes out and brings seven other spirits more evil than it is, and they go in and live there. So the person has even more trouble than before. It is the same way with the evil people who live today."*

The devil and his comrades are mad that they can't intimidate a true believer to give up their standard of living. Even people who don't want to come up in God while maturing in Christ will attempt to find ways to stop the leader from being successful in following God and doing His will in their life and the ministry God has called them to do. It is amazing to what lengths people who don't want others to be successful in their Christian walk with God will go to. They try to disconnect the leader from hearing God for their life, ministry, and family. They then try to knock the leader off focus and from being watchmen on the wall while trying to chase them out of His presence. All the while they are trying to make an excuse not to answer the call of God for their life in total obedience. It happened in Moses' day and is still happening now.

I'm not saying every leader is a perfect leader at all times. Like myself, remembering when I started God called me to start my first church and God knows He was birthing some things out of me. Believe me the saying is real, "Great man make mistakes! But they learn from them and arise to be stronger and better." I have made errors concerning some things in my past life.

All leaders have made mistakes before. It was when all of us had just been called, chosen, anointed and appointed as leaders. I don't care how you look at it right or wrong, the church is called to cover and pray for those who are diligently seeking and serving God. When their moment or test comes, the Church is called to encourage the leader to keep him standing. But, in this hour you have people assisting devils (demonic spirits) in the church. These demonic spirits will use people to encourage the pastor to go ahead and sin in his weak state or to give up and turn away from the vision and mission of God. These people controlled by demonic spirits don't want to come out of bondage or take the responsibility of answering the commands and demands of God.

Just like the players in football are supposed to cover the quarterback or runner with the ball without condition, so the church is called to cover the leader and not get mad when things don't happen how they want or because the leader's eye is not on them to be first lady or first man. You don't turn the leader over to the enemy as bait or to Jezebel or Jesse-bel as my wife would collaborate. The thing I've learned from self-experience as a leader and pastor for almost a period of six years is that you need to watch who is in your circle and be careful and prayerful of who you allow in your circle of life and in your circle of ministry!

Exodus 28 talks about Aaron's new promotion and his new position as a high priest called by God. He was an assistant pastor to Moses. While Moses was on top of the mountain receiving instructions from God, the children of Israel, the first church, had encouraged Aaron to make them a false God. All this was happening before the commandments could be given and while God was telling Moses about the commandments and the promotion of Aaron. Aaron happened to be one of the most failing leaders there ever was in the Bible, yet he was still fit to be used in God's eyes.

When Moses returned off the mountain top, Aaron lied about the sin of the people in commanding that a calf be made for the people to worship. God uses imperfection to reveal His glory in perfection. God uses leaders who have made open mistakes to bring Him glory on earth by showing His love and kindness.

Through the humble leaders who can sympathize and feel the infirmities of the people while having compassion since he or she too was in the same pothole because of their past mistakes and disobedience to God at one point in their life. Now, they are living epistles that God's mercy and grace abounds all the more. So, if you know of anyone including yourself, who acts as if they have not sinned or made errors, then check everyone's Pamper because one may be dropping and leaking leaving a trail behind that you are unaware of for others to see.

In **Genesis 9:20-23** Noah became a farmer and planted a vineyard. The vineyard represents this present day God's kingdom builders and planters flowing in the apostolic anointing. He drank the wine from the grapes that he planted and lay naked in his tent, after being chosen to be the builder of the ark and then delivered from the flood. But one of his three sons, Ham, exposed him with his eyes and mouth telling his brothers of their father's shameful state. After hearing of their father's nakedness, Shem and Japheth, Noah's two mature sons, placed a shawl over their shoulders and backed into their father's tent dwelling and covered his nakedness. The shawl represents prayer and placing the shawl on their shoulders represents carrying the responsibility or burden. We are called to pray for our leaders, brother or sister, whom God has called in the midst of their folly to share His mighty love, goodness and compassion with others. It is a great responsibility, yet an honor and privilege, to stand in the gap for one's leader and others as directed by the Lord. Jesus stands in the gap for each one of us consistently.

Hebrews 7:25 *"He is able to save forever those who draw near to God through him, because he always lives to make intercession for them."*

For the Lord wishes no man to perish. If you think about it, if it had not been for Noah and some of today's leaders who are chosen and highly favored by God, the ones who God has privileged to walk or catch the spiritual ride with Him would be lost and stagnate drowning in a pool of sin.

If only God could find in this final hour, kingdom minded people who are willing to pray. I'm not talking about the preying that a lion does or the devil does when he seeks for something to prowl on. If the leaders called to the kingdom today could find just that one Joshua as God gave me, one faithful minister who did not fall to the wayside or betray me but who covered me and my children, holding my hands up spiritually while in battle despite my weakness or downer moments, before I was blessed with a wife of standard and virtue to pray me through. If in the Kingdom of God we could find a Joshua or Caleb to bear the men and women God has chosen and called for a work even when it looks like they are swaying to stand with their leader, the leader is mindful and watchful as we know there will always be a sideline devil and imposter lurking for a mistake or error to occur. You know the ones in the church that root for you to run the race but all the time in their heart they have their own intentions. They are jealous hoping you would fumble the ball so they could take your place and pick up where it looked like it was over for you because of your tiredness and weariness. On occasions, they try and knock you out of place and snatch their way in position, giving themselves the glory and not God the glory as that was always your intention and the reason that God chose you and not them. You willingly give God all honor and praise. I tell people everywhere when I travel to be careful who is in their ear, especially if they are talking about someone else whether in or out of the kingdom of God. They are supposed to be a child of God, and if they talk about them, they will surely turn in the end and talk about you, after they have used you to help their emotions to become self-justified for the hate and ungodly rage they possess.

For we are called to pray for one another even if someone was or is in a mess because eventually they will smell and see where they are and arise and come to their senses like the prodigal son in **Luke 15:11-32.**

In **John 13:17**, *"Jesus said I have come not to condemn the world but I have come that the world through Me may be saved."*

Isn't it like the enemy to use that which was close to you in a season to go dig up your past as he sees your future is bright in God? Just like these men Korah, Miriam, Aaron, and Judas were close to Moses, and Jesus, my enemies called DCF (Department of Children and Families) were making false accusations of abuse and neglect toward my children while slaying my name in the streets declaring that

I was not a pastor and so many other things that I gave God glory for. My name got to be known and my ministry became stronger as they were slaying me.

The ring leader and person who spoke such negative words and played the main part in the whole thing was a person who I had truly loved and helped out from being in a homeless state in the midst of my brokenness at the time of my life's vital state. This person had become bitter and evil because of their marriage not working, wanting to blame me for their mate's manipulating ways and how he'd turned the word of God around to suit his own gain. It was also because of jealousy and their mate admiring the God in me. In whom I stood with for a season and prayed for in the midst of wrong, as a pastor is called to do while bringing correction from the Lord for any of his sheep. At that time I had figured I could save a lot of people then, but if I had known what I know now, brother man and sister girl would have been standing alone in the fire of life. I'm quite sure they would say the same but thank God for that lesson learned. But I think I did what God would have had me do at the time despite who liked it or did not.

Jesus never left us in our ignorance. He stood and still stands with us even in the midst of us all having to reap what we sowed because of ignorance. But don't take his mercy for granted like some have and still are doing to this day.

I was a single father for almost a five year period and never had such said or done to me. But because of their self-righteousness and not being able to manipulate the man of God and not wanting to take responsibility for their own actions, they fought to try and block and stop me. The children of Israel did the same thing to Jeremiah, Ezekiel and the other men and women of God in the old days and nowadays, who declare God's word to a rebellious nation of people.

As I am on my way to see God and His glory at the top where He has ordered my steps while yet staying determined as God does a new thing in me, through me and around me consistently. I continue to stand firm through all of the plots of the enemy declaring God's word and my testimony of how He brought me through despite the haters and accusers. Even though falsely accused and set up to be hurt and destroyed by former associates, it all eventually turned and worked in my favor.

Isaiah 54:17 (NKJV) *"No weapon formed against you (or me) shall prosper, And every tongue which rises against you (and me) in judgment You (God) shall condemn. This is the heritage of the **servants** of the Lord, And their righteousness is from Me," Says the Lord."*

After this trial, blessings flowed to me and I found myself more anointed, stronger, wiser, and closer to the Lord in my prayer life, praise life, worship life and communication with God, my wife and children. A family that prays together does indeed stay together. After this trial and every other test I have had to walk through and be tried in, miracles took place for me and on behalf of my household. Each test also built more of God's character in me and taught me how to trust in God all the more while keeping my composure for His Glory as a husband, father, pastor, leader of integrity and a prophet to the nations.

While learning how to rest and trust in God knowing that I did not have to fight the battle as I used to as I would snap, crackle and pop off on someone quickly, taking matters into my own hands. The major lesson was forgiveness and love, learning how to walk in the office of a real priest, praying and interceding for them who know not what they do as Jesus said; but in my case, knowing what they did and were doing. I did learn the lesson I can say! I remember the Lord allowed me to see the young lady for whom I prayed for to get a transplant miracle. Years later she joined forces with Satan and his posy because of me having order and a standard about my life, thus rejecting her out of my life and no longer associating with her. This young lady went lying and slaying my name. My first thought when I was to meet with her was to knock her out. But thank God for the Holy Spirit and His leading, unctioning my wife and me to cry out for His mercy and grace about an hour before I saw her, not knowing that the crying out was so the God in me would take control of my flesh and emotions. When I saw this person and spoke to them, they could not say a thing, their mouth was mute.

The Lord ushered me over to them and I told them I forgave them and still loved them and hugged them. I told them to repent and ask for forgiveness. At the same time I told them God is going to judge them if they did not correct their wrong and continue running in pride. All of this came from the Holy Spirit and the love of God.

I could not believe I flowed in the Spirit of God in such mannerism. The person was really shocked, I believe. Even though in pride, they still refused to apologize and stood their mute like a dull faced mannequin.

After I departed from them, I prayed that she would repent before something comes upon her and she doesn't have the time to do so. The truth of the matter is we all are judged by our ways. We have to be according to God's word. *"All must reap what we sow."* It does state in God's word *"Touch not my anointed ones and do my prophet no harm."* So, if any of you have a problem with God's men servants, leave them to God. It would be detrimental for you to try and do them some harm. You will reap the judgments and the consequences in your life sooner or later in ways you'd least expect. It will have you wondering why you are working hard with a degree but still are not satisfied or happy and why your children have grown to be your enemy. Just to name a few reapers that occurred because of the death you sowed by your mouth toward God's chosen children. He will protect His real sheep that are sold out for the cause of His Kingdom who say 'yes'. It takes all that and then some to be kept from Satan and the love of the world.

In **Genesis 4:19-35**, the Bible stated Cain killed his brother and when asked by God where his brother was, Cain's pride responded and he stated *"Am I my brother's keeper?"* God then put His mark on him and cursed him and put him to an open shame in front of the people. Yet God told him if any man did him harm so the same shall be turned to him sevenfold.

To learn how to apply and yield to the call of God when confronted by your giant or enemy, please study the anointing of King David, as a prophet, priest, and king, when called as a leader. It will teach you and show you how to address every situation in the wilderness or stronghold that you might have or come against on the way to your palace and destiny in Christ.

In this life, sometimes it is who you have ministered to and have walked with for a season or maybe all your lifelong who will try to kill you. But, if only they had known it was the plot of Judas because of his ignorant, doubtful, selfish, and rebellious greedy spirit that got Jesus crucified in the flesh but yet glorified in the Spirit. I have learned when I am put into a situation that I should have acted in my flesh about, to look back and say thank you to my enemies. Your lies and plots in trying to hurt, block and stop me has only helped me to reach the top quicker, and to become a better steward of God and His Word; thus, being able to manifest the fruits of my life, helping me to check myself daily while aligning my walk with God's word. Some would have lost their mind and others would have taken vengeance themselves.

But me, I received and understood and learned the lesson God was teaching me. I learned how to rest in God and wait on the Lord as He made and is still making His enemies and mine our footstool.

I used to question God, why me? I am serving you. And He spoke to me telling me that it is your past and trials that I will use to get you to your future and your Judas to get Me glorified in your life. God had to teach me how to put my trust in Him and to trust no man, and how He needed to show the enemy, the accuser of the brethren, His power, and that it was He that redeemed me. It wasn't jail house religion. It was experiencing relationship with God, walking in obedience and being touched and filled with the Baptism of Fire and Holy Ghost.

After I made my transition out of bondage to becoming set free, I thought of how I was so foolish in letting my flesh and the enemy overthrow me and rule over me, running from the call of God for my life, not really knowing what I was doing.

Every time I thought of going to church or felt like I needed to pray or when I would close my spirit to God's children who were just passing by wanting to minister God's love, grace and mercy to me in the midst of my foolishness and bound state. This is what happens to you when you don't know Jesus as your Lord and personal Savior.

Wanting real life will cause you to lose yours whether it is spiritual or physical. This is what the demon possessed man must have realized in his wilderness. Before I got saved, the transition to hell was a work that I had learned. The transition to eternal life is a work, as well. Which will you choose?

Living in a world that contradicts itself is a world blinded by death. Being around negative influences is a circle and trench leading to death.

Notice the state of the demon possessed man, all his mind and body was subject to the enemy, the devil. He had allowed what he was dealing with mentally to affect him spiritually causing him to be infected physically. Not knowing what to do or where to turn and having no safe haven, he lost control emotionally, causing him to faint and give up, leaving a portal for the enemy to possess his body, mind and soul. There was then no fighting spirit of standard and perseverance left in him. He didn't know what to do or where to go....living a life in limbo.

Luke 8:29 (NKJV) *"For he had commanded the unclean spirit to come out of the man. For it had often seized him, and he was kept under guard, bound with chains and shackles; He broke the bonds and was driven by the demon in the wilderness"*

Now if you look at verse 28 you find Jesus spoke to one spirit commanding it to leave; but now you see in verses 26-27that he had many demons for a long time in his life. The major event that had happened to this man allowed many spiritual doors to be opened and to remain open allowing many demonic spirits entrance to control him in the transition of his life. Kinda like a schizophrenic. The demons drove this man to a place where no one would come in contact with or bother this vessel they had possessed. They had him where they wanted him, in an unknown and uncontrollable place so they could control him taking full advantage of him. Many people feared and dreaded the region that the man was driven to but the demons were more fearful as they did NOT want to be kicked out or cast out of this man's life, nor did they want anyone to be able to give him a word of hope, setting him free. If you noticed the places where church goers, not kingdom minded people, complain is when God directs them or the body of Christ into the wilderness, to learn, mature and exercise their God given authority.

In **Matthew chapter 3** we find that John the Baptist dwelt in the wilderness eating locusts and wild honey, preaching repentance. But we find that the demons drove this man into the wilderness as well. Well, if God sends men there, why did the demons drive him there? I will tell you why, demons know that without God and His Word we are defeated in the wilderness. Demons also knew at this time that religious leaders didn't understand that the wilderness is where God builds his people and their faith, exercising the word of God in them. Isn't it funny how the devil studies to show himself approved to defeat us? But we have some Christians today who are just

Christians doing nothing to advance in God's kingdom, not wanting to go through, learning how to exercise their faith, word and gifts in the wilderness facing the enemy so they may defeat him.

The Pharisees and Sadducees were using and turning God's word for their own gain. They had not experienced walking with God in the dark and dry places, nor the suffering of this present age. In other words, they were just talk and had a form of a Godly walk. The Pharisees and Sadducees had no relationship with God or Jesus where they would be able to testify and have a testimony to share in order to bring and direct others out. So they had no power over death or the enemy to bring deliverance or healing to the body of Christ. That's why there was a rage in them when Jesus came preaching and teaching and bringing the word with demonstration and power. After Jesus was baptized, filled by the Holy Spirit and driven by the Holy Spirit to walk through the wilderness for forty days and forty nights being tried by the devil, He came back filled with power and authority. (**Matthew 4:1-11**)

In **Mark 6:30-33** you read that Jesus went through the cities and towns preaching and healing; but He also went to the deserted places, where many came to see Him.

This is a place where immature Christians don't like to vacation for spiritual and mental growth because they are challenged to live on God's word, living on their faith, causing them to let go and let God take control.

Luke 8:30 (NKJV) *"Jesus then asked him, saying, "what is your name?" And he said, "Legion" because many demons had entered him."*

Luke 8:31 (NKJV) *"And they begged Him that He would not cast them out into the abyss."*

Jesus asked the man what is his name due to his mental and physical condition, after he commands the spirit out of him. Who are you? What is your position? Where do you belong? In order for one to come to terms of reality, they must know who they are in life and where their life is taking them knowing they have control.

You find this spirit speaks and says we are legions meaning many. In this man's past he had gotten into some really bad situations or circumstances and had contact with the wrong people. These people had some demons too from bad experiences that rubbed off onto him. Or should we say that were deposited on him causing numerous spirits to enter him giving him multiple personalities, mixed emotions, causing breakdowns and possibly some break ups in his spiritual being and tangible life. So now you find him not only carrying his own demons but demons from others he has had contact with or an encounter with.

I have seen a lot of people come to my church where I pastor, who played G.I. Joe. They would reach out to help everyone else in deep dark despair, looking and seeming to love without condition, but inside they were in deep dark waters of unhappiness. They had not been delivered.

Looking to make someone else happy they thought would make them happy; thinking that by their good works it would get rid of their issues thus bringing deliverance, peace and consistent happiness. They would go home carrying the mental and spiritual problems of others while still battling their own. Not knowing how to handle the situation caused it to just linger putting them into a deeper depression and so much more stress. The stress and depression had increased tremendously inside of them where it had gotten to the point of them living and sleeping in dark rooms and having unstable thoughts of suicide and delusions. Some even picked up more stress on the job from coworkers, along with the complaints of family and friends through telephone or home visits, forcing them into the same spiritual bind and stronghold. One minute they were up and the next down, feeling free then back to feeling bound.

This is a sign of being tormented by spirits of darkness. Jesus keeps you in a state of oneness of mind, with Him giving you peace. He has you feeling and believing that you are more than a conqueror in Him. You will feel like you are able to accomplish anything that others only dare to dream of or do. This is why it is so important that once you are saved that you have a relationship with God. You must maintain focus on building a pure and holy oneness, a solid foundation in Him, being one with Him; thus, obtaining balance and order within your life while directing others to Jesus as He is the one and only true Savior.

Tragedy Turned to Treasure

Luke 8:38 (NKJV), *"now the man from whom the demons had departed begged Him that he might be with Him. But Jesus sent him away saying,"*

Luke 8:39 (NKJV), *"Return to your own house, and tell what great things God has done for you". And he went his way and proclaimed throughout the whole city what great things Jesus had done for him."*

In this passage of scripture, you read that Jesus would not allow the once demon possessed man to come follow Him and His ministry, making him a disciple, but He used him to reach those where He had been uninvited. In **Luke 8:39** it states the man went his way and proclaimed what great things Jesus had done for him. Now, he went his way means that he had a different ministry or had a different way to reach the people. Besides, he was from the region and who knows their own people better than the person who is from there.

This man reached those who Jesus could not get to because of men, their greed and pride of life. What better testimony is there than when a person everyone knew to be a minus to society, a viscous threat and a nobody goes and shows the glory of God and how His grace has come upon their life. Thus, saving them bringing healing and deliverance unto their mind, soul and spirit and freeing them back to their right state of mind. Jesus also saw the man's willingness to be used, not staying stuck in a place where the enemy would find him again. So to exercise his gifts and the ministry he had now obtained after his date with destiny and deliverance, Jesus directed him back with a new outlook on life.

After this encounter with Jesus, this man now understood that he had purpose and meaning. Now, he could face the same situations and circumstances but handle them differently, knowing that he would face the same old people who had given up on him leaving him for dead.

Jesus knew that if they had seen him that was once bound, now loosed; him that was down, now up; and him that was enslaved, now free, that those same old people who assisted the devil were the same old people that would have to deny the devil and his blinding them and now open their eyes, believe and glorify

God. That is why one is not to be ashamed of where God has brought them from and delivered them out of. Every man on earth has done something or is doing something that has traumatized himself or stagnated himself, causing him to be a walking zombie or it will traumatize him causing him to be a walking corpse. He used to and may still be pondering as to whether anyone knows his little secret. Has it become open or is it still secret? The fact of the matter is that God has come not to condemn the world but that through His Son, Jesus, many might be saved.

I remember when God used me after my release from prison. He sent me right back among the same old people who knew me, and everything I used to do. And "boy" did it exercise my level of integrity, worship, praise, and prayer life. It caused my ministry to soar. Not only did I have to face my past as Moses did when he murdered the Egyptian, but I had to learn how to allow God to mend and deal with all the brokenness, hurt and shame.

I remember the Lord spoke to me upon my being released saying, "The ones who loved you in your past will hate you and the ones who hated you will love you." I started thinking, why God would say something like that. Well, He was right! Those who I was close to called me all kinds of name from fake to false and much more behind my back. And those who didn't like me were the people who supported my ministry the most by giving money, sending prayer, and calling every day to check on me.

Before God sent me into full time ministry, He brought me low and taught me how to deal with my inner self, my emotions, and then how to defeat the enemy. Walking upright and in love while forgiving myself as He forgave me, killing the enemy with kindness.

I learned resting in Him and not being moved by people or situations was the key.

I was a traveling Prophet, being invited to different churches, prophesying life over many as I did in prison. You know with God, He does use the foolish things to confound the wise. I took a lot of time out over the years in meditation thinking on my past and some of the events that occurred. Then at some point I would ask God why I had allowed the enemy to control my life for a season. The Lord spoke saying because you had a lot of Jacob role models in your life. (Jacob means deceiver.) But these Jacobs never got tired of roaming in the desert and never got to the point of life that they needed to face who they were and wrestle with Me for a new name and spirit. The root of evil starts somewhere, so watch, as well as pray, like Jesus commanded.

The first places God opened a door for me to preach in were in my hometown. I was working at Sonny's Barbeque and this pastor that I had seen on television walked in. I said "I know you from television." He and his wife greeted me and we talked. He invited me to come testify at his church the following week. Then God opened a door and sent me while I was, yet, a Minister traveling to Miami, Florida, a place I grew up in. The power of God was present because of my willingness to go, say, and do what God desired and my obedient lifestyle to and before Him. This opportunity came while yet a minister working at a hotel in my hometown. This now, Bishop was staying there with a few of her members getting ready to go to a conference at the Pastor's church whom I had met while working at Sonny's Barbeque. They stopped me in the hallway and began to speak with me.

I then allowed the Lord to use me to speak prophetically over them. Then, they began to tell me about their pastor, who arrived moments later. We had a Holy Ghost time right there by the elevators at my job while I was on my way pushing a cart with some sheets to the laundry room. We prophesied life into one another.

Before I knew it, the following year God had me right there in Miami, the place I grew up in preaching, teaching, singing, healing, and prophesying the gospel of Jesus Christ. He allowed me to go back where I came from to bring others out of the state of bondage so that He would get the glory. God's word and my testimony flowed out of me by the power of the Holy Ghost like water. The people were shouting, falling out, and dancing. I remember speaking of how I was placed on television around the world years back for stealing a beautiful thoroughbred horse.

They placed me on the news a day after being incarcerated. The pod I was in at that very time was watching the news channel and there my face appeared. While I was in jail inmates asked me what I was going to do with the horse. I said the same thing that you do when you get your drugs; you smoke it, snort it, or sell it. In my case, I was going to ride it and sell it. The devil had me bound. I was so ashamed of myself in jail that day and making the national news because every inmate looked back at me. You could hear them asking, saying is that him? Then they questioned me.

When asked by an inmate, I would say, you shouldn't question me, you better question yourself and your lawyer so when the officers come to take you before the Judge, you can defend your crimes. I was just embarrassed, that's all. People talk biggity (smart) as the old folks say, when they know they are guilty or in the wrong and don't want to face or acknowledge they are wrong and need help to come out of their mental and spiritual bondage.

When I got out on bond, I was too ashamed to go to the stores or around anyone that I thought had known my face. It didn't stop me from stealing though. It was off to the races again. I stole more cars, and wrote more bad checks than I could count. Today that in which I had no control over, being demonically possessed at the time and bound with the yokes of iniquity, has happened to turn and become a major testimony for me.

Helping people to become free, open and honest, and to know who Christ is and that power is in the blood Jesus shed on Calvary.

It also gives people a good laugh. In the back of their minds I can hear them say, "Thank God, I was not the only fool out there." Especially, when I tell them how the devil had me so fooled that when I stole the horse that I walked it so far in the middle of the night, to the place I was taking it which was forty miles to be exact with no water to give it. The horse kept laying down. At first I could, pop it on its butt to get it to stand back up so we could continue on walking, but after a while it laid down and wouldn't get up for minutes even if I popped it on its butt. I could imagine that horse was saying, "You're just going to have to keep hitting me, because you're not going to kill me, fool! Where is the water at?" I own my own horses now. That is right horses with an "s" and I got them by the favor of God on my life.

Thank You, Jesus! Who would have thought a man from my background would possess such power and authority, along with success and prosperity in the Spirit and in the earth realm because of God and His favor on my life. The things many have done in life are crazy. If we allow life and its pollution to affect us, we will become victims of it.

The devil told me that I would never be anything because of the events that had taken place in my life, not having a father around twenty-four seven, seeing my Mom struggle to raise me, coming from a background of a broken un-oriented family and being a high school dropout. I allowed the enemy to tell me that I had no future because of my education level. At some point in my growing up years, I wanted people to acknowledge that I existed on earth because of the love that I lacked as a child. All I wanted at the time was to know what real love was and how it felt to get rid of the void of darkness that lingered in the pit of my stomach. I was a young man who would do whatever for a moment of love and to temporarily fill the emptiness.

At one point in my life I felt that I had let everyone around me down and was a disgrace, after all I had done as a criminal and a conman. While growing up to become a man, I held on to others not wanting to associate with me or be around me as many made fun of me. But as I got saved, I understood that it was a part of the call. Prophets are different and are called to walk alone!

I remember I used to wear suspenders, penny loafers, thick white socks, and this blue jean jacket to school in the middle of the August heat. Was I ever picked at and picked on. My grandmother thought I was so handsome, dressing me like a country backyard preacher in casual wear and in dress shoes.

You have to be careful letting your loved ones set you up to fall in the den of lions. It helps to be different in the long run. Now, with me owning my own clothing line, people are wearing my designer clothing all over the United States where I have toured over the past couple of years.

I thank God He saved and delivered me. The healing was a process though, and the forgiveness part I had to learn. People forgave me, but most importantly God forgave me even before they forgave me or before I learned to forgive myself. But, thank God I have learned the lesson of forgiveness. I have also learned not to be the devil's doormat and never to be anybody's fool. You can forgive. But, never forget until the person is saved and is walking the straight and narrow, preparing the way of the Lord to come, allowing God to continually change and soften their heart of stone to a heart of flesh, or else they might still

put a dagger in you and through you,
unknowingly.

Made in the USA
Columbia, SC
29 June 2019